Original title:
The Arbor Awakens

Copyright © 2025 Creative Arts Management OÜ
All rights reserved.

Author: Helena Marchant
ISBN HARDBACK: 978-1-80567-068-1
ISBN PAPERBACK: 978-1-80567-148-0

Ancients Stirring in the Light

In the bark, old stories flat,
Leaves gossip like a fuzzy cat.
Roots do yoga, stretch and flex,
While the branches play complex.

Squirrels giggle, swap their hats,
In the shade, the chipmunk chats.
Wisdom laughs from boughs so wise,
Telling tales to passing skies.

Sunlight Dances on Leafy Dreams

Sunbeams waltz on blades of grass,
While shadows cheer, they hop and pass.
Dandelions wear their crowns, bold,
Telling secrets to the old gold.

The daisies dance, they twirl with glee,
As butterflies join the jamboree.
Laughter rustles through the green,
As nature hosts a lively scene.

The Return of the Verdant Spirit

A sprout pokes up its cheeky head,
Tickling toes, it plays instead.
Gathering dew for breakfast fun,
Grinning wide beneath the sun.

Old oaks chuckle, swaying slow,
Whispering jokes that only they know.
Moss plays games with passing feet,
Nature's pranks are hard to beat!

Awakening in Nature's Embrace

Buds pop open with a cheer,
Tiny voices shout, 'We're here!'
The grasshoppers huff and puff,
While ladybugs strut, looking tough.

Clouds tumble, tickling the pines,
As silly squirrels make funny signs.
Morning breaks with giggles and glee,
A raucous party for you and me.

Treetops in Tender Hues

Up in the branches, squirrels dance,
Throwing acorns like a wild romance.
Leaves burst forth in a silly spree,
What a day for a tree jubilee!

Bees are buzzing, buzzing loud,
As trees sway in the giggling crowd.
A woodpecker joins with a peck and a knock,
Tapping out a tune, a merry mock!

The flowers blurt out in colors bold,
Their petals tickle with stories untold.
A frog in a top hat hops with glee,
To join the party beneath the free!

With nature's jokes as the backdrop play,
Life returns in a whimsical display.
Branches shrug off the winter's glaze,
As they twirl in a fragrant, leafy praise!

Chronicles of the Woodland Revival

Once were the trees, a gloomy sight,
Now they're sprouting in sheer delight.
Chipmunks chatter, trying to outsmart,
Every leaf that tickles their heart.

Mushrooms wear hats, so silly and round,
Frolicking fairies weave laughs all around.
The pine cones giggle, a playful team,
Growing together like a woodland dream.

From the ground up, the grass joins in,
Bouncing along, with a cheeky grin.
Saplings share secrets, gossiping fast,
Wondering how long the joy can last.

With each passing breeze, the laughter grows,
As critters invent their own funny shows.
In this enchanted, rib-tickling realm,
Nature takes charge; it's her funny helm!

Spheres of Light within the Boughs

In the thick woods, a radiant glow,
Tickled by sunbeams, putting on a show.
Fireflies gather, wearing tiny hats,
Twinkling like stars, chubby and fat.

Whimsical shadows dance on the ground,
Chasing their tails, in a merry round.
A deer takes a leap, almost a prance,
Who knew that trees were masters of dance?

Laughter echoes from canopy high,
As birds crack jokes beneath the blue sky.
A rabbit chuckles, munching on a leaf,
Declaring himself the arboreal chief!

Bubbles of light make the branches beam,
Nature's wonders blend into a dream.
In this zany place where silliness thrives,
Joy bounces forth, and laughter survives!

The Resurrection of the Green

Once clad in grey, now dressed in bright,
The trees brush off the sleep, what a sight!
Caterpillars wiggle in jubilant cheer,
Turning into butterflies, oh dear, oh dear!

Blossoms burst with giggles and sighs,
While beetles march in tiny ties.
Squirrels play tag, with endless zest,
Claiming the branches, they're simply the best.

A hearty chorus of croaks and squeaks,
As nature unveils her playful peaks.
The earth laughs back, a joyous sound,
With colors exploding all around!

Through shimmering leaves, the laughter flows,
As life springs forth, with merry throes.
In this playground where green likes to joke,
Nature's revival is no hoax!

Enchantment of the Flourishing Glade

In a glade where squirrels prance,
The mushrooms wear hats, they dance.
The rabbits play hide-and-seek,
While owls gossip, so to speak.

The flowers gossip, pink and blue,
They chat about the morning dew.
Bumblebees join in the fun,
Performing tricks just for the sun.

A frog croaks jokes, quite absurd,
His punchline's lost—a little blurred.
But laughter echoes through the trees,
Even the ants giggle with ease.

The stream's a mirror, shiny bright,
Reflecting all this pure delight.
In this glade where antics reign,
Nature's charm is quite insane.

New Lives in the Shade

Under leaves, a mystery blooms,
Tiny critters dodge their dooms.
A lizard slips, a squirrel slips too,
While beetles march in a line of blue.

In whispers soft, the shadows tease,
Telling tales to the rustling breeze.
Chubby worms in silly hats,
Argue fiercely with the chats.

Sunbeams peek, cast silly rays,
On fuzzy bunnies in their plays.
Each acorn drops, a joke in disguise,
Nature's humor, oh, how it flies!

The shade is ripe with mischievous glee,
As bright parades of ants agree.
With every leaf a laugh is brewed,
In the laughter of the woodlands' mood.

Forest of the Expected

In the woods, where gnomes reside,
Their noses twitch, their eyes so wide.
They wait for tea parties to commence,
But squirrels sneak in—what a suspense!

A tree stump wears a welcome mat,
As chipmunks scurry, and shadows chat.
Leaves perform a jig with grace,
While badgers roll, just in place.

Pine cones drop with thundering claps,
They land on heads, despite the traps.
Yet giggles rise from every nook,
It's a forest full of a funny book.

Dancing branches sway and tease,
As fireflies dart like little bees.
With every step, surprise awaits,
In the forest where fun elates.

Dawn's Light over Resilient Roots

With dawn comes laughter, bright and loud,
As sun strikes leaves, they laugh out proud.
The roots below are tickled so,
By worms that wiggle to and fro.

At sunrise, crickets sing in tune,
While frogs wear crowns and beam at the moon.
A fox jogs past in a funny way,
Chasing shadows that run astray.

The morning dew drips like a joke,
As every creature giggles, bespoke.
A family of owls having brunch,
While squirrels play leap, then munch.

In this realm of giggles and cheer,
Every dawn brings a fun frontier.
With bright smiles creeping through the woods,
It's a world where laughter always broods.

Luminescent Life in Hidden Hollows

In deep, dark corners critters scheme,
A raccoon dons a captain's beam.
With fireflies, he starts a race,
While squirrels laugh and shake their face.

A frog recites with all his charm,
Nearby, his friend, the lizard's calm.
They toast to night with bugs for snacks,
And dance beneath the twinkling cracks.

Vibrant Life in Slumber's Wake

Awake! Awoke! The hedgehogs shout,
As butterflies spin round about.
A sleepy deer just rolls its eyes,
While grasshoppers practice their high-fly tries.

The pinecone laughs, cracks a joke,
About the worm that dreamed of smoke.
Each twig and leaf begins to giggle,
As morning time makes shadows wriggle.

Rise of the Woodland Spirits

Woodland sprites with merry glee,
Wiggle their toes in harmony.
They play tricks with the morning mist,
And hide behind the trees, persist.

A dandelion's fluff floats by,
Like little fairies in the sky.
With giggles loud and whispers sweet,
They're dancing on their tiny feet.

Color and Sound of Awakening Woods

The dawn erupts in vibrant hues,
As chatty birds exchange their news.
A bear in pajamas yawns and wakes,
While knocking over all the cakes.

The brook just laughs, a bubbly friend,
As nature's pranks seem never end.
With colors bright and laughter loud,
The woods rejoice, a lively crowd.

Flicker of Hope in Leafy Spaces

In the shade where squirrels prance,
Tiny buds begin to dance.
A bumblebee with a tiny hat,
Whispers secrets to a sleeping rat.

Sunlight tickles blades of grass,
As the ants march in a class.
A ladybug, with spots so bold,
Shares gossip 'bout the flowers' gold.

Dance of the Sprouts

Tiny sprouts in a wobbly row,
Struggling hard, but what a show!
One tips over, giggles sprout,
While worms cheer them on, no doubt!

Frogs take bets on who will grow,
Giant radish, or green avocado?
With each stretch and every wiggle,
Nature keeps us all in giggle.

Fresh Beginnings in the Quiet

First morning light, the leaves all sway,
Rustling whispers, 'Let's seize the day!'
A fluffy bunny with a wobbly nose,
Plucks a dandelion and inadvertently doze.

A snail crawls, in style sleek,
Wearing a shell, peerless mystique.
'Is it a hat or a tiny home?'
He chuckles softly, 'I'll never roam!'

When Seasons Shift in the Thicket

As winter bids a friendly goodbye,
The trees giggle and start to sigh.
With sprigs of green and a dash of fun,
Elves play hide and seek on the run.

A chipmunk sports a snazzy scarf,
While flowers bloom and trees just laugh.
'What a season to shake and cheer!'
Nature's comedy, oh so dear!

Song of the Swaying Branches

Branches giggle, swaying to and fro,
Tickling the clouds, putting on a show.
Squirrels dance in a wild ballet,
While the leaves shout, 'Hip hooray!'

Breezes chuckle, playing peek-a-boo,
As acorns drop, a game just for you.
The trunks do wiggle, a funny sight,
Roots twist and turn, full of delight.

Echoing Through the Timbered Realm

Echoes bounce, giggles fill the air,
Woodpeckers drum without a care.
With every tap, they spread the cheer,
A chuckling concert, woodlands near.

Branches gossip, whispering their tales,
Of mischief done by their leafy trails.
A frog joins in, croaking its song,
As butterflies flutter, dancing along.

A Tapestry of Green

Woven in shades of laughter and cheer,
Dandelions weave, jumping here and there.
A patch of moss wears a fuzzy hat,
While butterflies giggle, on a leaf they sat.

The ferns sway like they're skipping rope,
Mushrooms pop up, giving a yelp of hope.
In this quilt, every creature plays,
Nature's humor brightens our days.

Enchanted Canopies Awaken

Canopies chuckle, lifting their crowns,
As chipmunks race up without any frowns.
Sunlight tickles through leafy gates,
While the branches dance, oh how it grates!

As shadows play hide and seek with joy,
A happy breeze whispers, 'Oh boy, oh boy!'
With every rustle, a story unfolds,
A woodland jest, forever retold.

Songs of the Soaring Boughs

In the treetops, squirrels dance,
Chasing tails in a silly prance.
Birds join in with their weird songs,
Nature hums where the fun belongs.

A raccoon dons a tiny crown,
Pretends he's king of this leafy town.
With acorns tucked beneath his paws,
He rules the branches without a pause.

The woodpecker's a clumsy chef,
Knocking on wood till there's none left.
He laughs and cackles, what a sight,
While ants march on in sheer delight.

A hippo tried to climb a tree,
Got stuck while laughing, oh so free.
Lifted by friends in a wobbly way,
They all cheered for him at the end of the day.

Mosaic of the Wooded Heart

Among the trunks, the shadows play,
Where frogs croak jokes about the day.
Lizards strut in silly fashion,
Creating bursts of joyous passion.

A hedgehog rolls with a comic flair,
A tumble here, then a tumble there.
While butterflies giggle in the air,
At how he spins without a care.

Underneath the leafy sprawl,
A party's brewing, come one, come all!
With mushrooms piled like birthday cakes,
And laughter echoing by the lakes.

Wise old owls in glasses so thick,
Declare they're hip, but we know the trick.
They share tales of the years gone by,
Turning wise sentences to silly sighs.

Whispers of the Awakening Grove

In a grove, the trees all chatter,
About how squirrels make them scatter.
With acorns dropped as gifts of cheer,
And giggles ringing far and near.

A chubby rabbit hops with grace,
Trying hard to keep his pace.
He trips and lands in a ferny bed,
Then mumbles softly, "Oops!" instead.

Beneath the branches, shadows spin,
With raccoon pranks and geese that grin.
They tell tall tales of their last feast,
Inviting all, both wild and beast.

The sun peeks through, a golden beam,
Awakening a laughter dream.
In every rustle, joy is found,
As smiles linger all around.

Echoes Beneath the Canopy

Underneath the shady leaves,
A chorus of giggles drifts and weaves.
The frogs provide the rhythmic beat,
As squirrels join in with tiny feet.

An owl hoots, trying hard to rhyme,
But ends up mixing words every time.
His friends roll about, in stitches of glee,
"You're the best comedian here," they agree.

A chipmunk juggles with some nuts,
While a deer looks on and quietly struts.
They cheer him on with a friendly clap,
Creating fun, a whimsical map.

As twilight falls with a playful sigh,
The moon winks down, a watchful eye.
In the forest, the laughter stays,
Echoing softly in the night's embrace.

Rebirth of the Whispering Trees

The trees stood tall with sleepy eyes,
Yawning wide beneath the skies.
They stretched their limbs with a big grin,
Swaying, laughing—let the fun begin!

The chirpy birds began to tease,
Dancing 'round with the buzzing bees.
A squirrel slipped on dew-kissed bark,
Fell with a bounce, oh what a lark!

Roots were tickled by the ticklish grass,
With every giggle, the time did pass.
Even the owls joined in the jest,
Hooting loudly, they know best!

So come and play in this leafy spree,
Where joy abounds from tree to tree.
In this silly forest of evergreen,
Nature's humor reigns pristine!

Songs of the Rejuvenated Canopy

The leaves rustled with a hearty laugh,
Singing tunes like a forest staff.
Branches swayed to a cheerful beat,
While critters joined in, oh what a treat!

A chorus formed with every breeze,
Echoes dancing through the trees.
Pitchy frogs with their croaks devised,
A funny song, so well disguised!

In the shade, a party brewed,
With acorns scattered, all were wooed.
The bark of laughter floated high,
While clouds above giggled in the sky!

So let us celebrate, don't be shy,
Lift your voice, let your spirits fly.
In this forest where mirth prevails,
Joyful songs fill the grand trails!

Life Breaches the Bark

Beneath the bark, a tickle grew,
A burst of green poked out, who knew?
Little sprouts with cheerful grins,
Competing in games no one wins!

A tiny bud claimed it would sprout,
While others argued about and about.
Who knew that greenery could be so loud,
In this woodsy crowd, we're all so proud!

Rabbits joined in, hopping with glee,
Challenging flowers to a dance spree.
Petals twirled like ballerinas fine,
As critters cheered, "Look at us shine!"

So watch for life in its playful form,
Through the laughter, the forest will warm.
With sprouts aloft reaching for the sky,
Together we jest, you and I!

The Forest's Heartbeat Quickens

The forest felt a joyful thrum,
A rhythm that made all hearts hum.
From the mushrooms to the tallest pine,
Every creature knew it was time to shine!

The rabbits threw a grand parade,
While mushrooms joined, unafraid.
With twirls and hops, they danced away,
Creating magic, come what may!

Even the stones began to jig,
In harmony with the critters big.
The breezes whispered silly secrets,
Leaving behind their playful regrets.

So let us skip through this bouncing land,
Where laughter grows, all are hand in hand.
In the thicket where spirits unite,
Laughter echoes, a pure delight!

Heroes of the Hidden Grove

In the grove where squirrels play,
The acorns roll, oh what a day!
A raccoon dons a tiny hat,
He claims he's now the forest's brat.

The owls gossip with great delight,
About the frogs who leap at night.
A chipmunk juggles berries round,
While giggling trees make silly sounds.

The bunnies dance on hidden trails,
In shoes made from old, worn-outails.
A wise old fox cracks jokes so sly,
While brushing off a spider's lie.

As sunlight streams through leafy rooms,
The giggles stir amid the blooms.
In this grove of joyful cheer,
The fauna plan a grand debut here!

Songs Born from Swelling Seeds

From the soil sprouts tunes of glee,
A flower sings, oh listen, see!
The daisies dance, the dandelions sway,
Each note a joy that brightens the day.

Bees buzzing loudly, in perfect tune,
Scare off the ants who dance to the moon.
The wind whispers jokes to the shyest buds,
While laughter rolls like playful floods.

Acorns rapping like tiny drums,
In harmony with the tapping thumbs.
The roots make beats, the leaves all clap,
As nature's kids take a happy nap.

Oh what a sight, the forest groove,
Spin 'round, jump up, get in the move!
Songs sprout up from every seed,
In this old wood, we plant our deed!

The Harmonies of Nature's Renewal

As springs arrive, the creek runs wild,
The frogs leap high, oh what a child!
A turtle joins the merry band,
Adventures planned, a day so grand.

The sun winks down, the petals cheer,
While shadows dance in the bright atmosphere.
The wise old oak tells stories funny,
Of nutty squirrels who chase the honey.

Butterflies twirl in the midday light,
With grasshoppers sharing jokes in flight.
The flowers giggle, tickled by bees,
As they sway gently with the beloved breeze.

In every corner, laughter rings,
Joy sprouts high on happy springs.
This nature folksy, smiling scene,
Renewal comes with a playful sheen!

Renewal in the Old Woods

In the woods, the squirrels dance,
Mossy hats and no pants.
Tree trunks giggle, roots do shake,
A concert for a laughing snake.

Old leaves whisper, 'What a show!'
Bunnies hop, putting on a faux glow.
The mushrooms start to sway and clap,
As fireflies join for a nightcap.

The owls hoot in bright surprise,
While chipmunks wear their best ties.
The ancient trees begin to cheer,
For every critter of good cheer.

Whispers echo, 'Don't be shy!'
Let's all join in! Come give it a try!
With leafy grins, they break from rest,
In the woods, they're simply blessed.

Roots Remembering Spring

The roots grumble, 'Time to wake!'
Forget the frost, for goodness' sake!
They wiggle and squirm beneath the ground,
Telling secrets of wonders found.

A beetle shouts, 'I slept like a log!'
While worms giggle, pulling a hog.
'What's next?' asks a curious sprout,
'Are we up for a new shout-out?'

The daisies burst out in a tease,
'We've got sun, why not a breeze?'
Frogs croak out a silly tune,
Promising fun from morn till noon.

With a rustle, the roots do sway,
'Bring on the laughter of each day!'
They lift their heads, ready to play,
As spring smiles in its own quirky way.

Blossoms of a New Dawn

Morning giggles in soft light,
Blossoms stretch with all their might.
Petals yawn and start to dance,
Bees all buzz in a happy trance.

Tulips tease with colors bright,
Waving flags, oh what a sight!
Sunbeams splash like paint on trees,
Dancing with a gentle breeze.

The daffodils have jokes to share,
'Knock, knock!' echoes in the air.
Butterflies play tag with the flies,
While poppies wear their brightest guise.

With each bloom, giggles resound,
In the garden, joy's unbound.
A showcase of flora, they perform,
A riot of colors in tangled form.

Secrets of the Slumbering Forest

Deep in the woods where shadows bask,
The trees have secrets, if you dare ask.
They chuckle low, with branches wide,
Sharing tales of those who've tried.

The raccoons plot with sneaky grins,
While ants perform their tiny spins.
Chipmunks whisper, 'Did you hear?'
A tale of a brave squirrel with no fear.

Mossy carpets hold a jest,
As owls hoot, they take a rest.
In this nook where laughter hides,
Even the shadows join the rides.

One secret told, the forest sighs,
A symphony of quirky highs.
With every rustle, giggles flowed,
In the heart of nature's abode.

Echoing Life Among Ancient Boughs

In the forest where squirrels dance,
Branches sway in a silly trance.
Birds gossip about the weather,
While turtles move, slow as a feather.

The owls squawk with great delight,
Chasing shadows in the fading light.
Rabbits jump in a comical spree,
Painting stripes on the old oak tree.

A raccoon juggles acorns with flair,
As chipmunks giggle without a care.
The wind whispers a playful tune,
Under the watch of the cheeky moon.

Life echoes in a joyful spree,
Amidst the laughter of the leafy spree.
Each bough, a stage for nature's play,
In the woods, where silliness holds sway.

A Lullaby for the Sleeping Woods

Hush now, little leaves don't sway,
The trees are ready for a snooze today.
Squirrels snore in their leafy beds,
While crickets dream with silly heads.

A bear hums a tune soft and low,
As fireflies twinkle like stars in a row.
Bunnies yawn with exaggerated grace,
In the world of dreams, they find their place.

The moon giggles at sleepy sights,
With owls sharing hilarious nights.
Dancing shadows tickle the ground,
In this peaceful retreat where joy is found.

Lullabies weave through branches high,
As stars wink down from the velvet sky.
The woods may sleep, but fun's on the rise,
In the embrace of the moonlit skies.

Renewal's Caress on the Tender Leaves

Springtime arrives with a playful wink,
As saplings sip dew from the brink.
Leaves giggle as they stretch up high,
Trying to tickle the clouds in the sky.

Buds burst forth with a comical cheer,
Each bloom swaying, shifting near.
Bees buzz by with a silly hum,
While butterflies join the joyful drum.

Worms wiggle in a dance on the ground,
Putting on a show without a sound.
Chirping birds join in with flair,
Each note giggling through the fair air.

Tender shoots laugh with all their might,
In this rebirth, they find delight.
Nature's embrace, silly and sweet,
Brings laughter to every sprouting feat.

Symphony of New Growth

Branches rustle, a musical play,
In the woods, where the young buds sway.
Tiny sprouts sing in tunes so bright,
Making melodies beneath the light.

Frogs croak a rhythm, offbeat and free,
As cattails sway with comical glee.
The gentle breeze joins in the song,
Creating a chorus where all belong.

Saplings sway to the drums of the earth,
Celebrating the joy of their birth.
With each rustle and flutter, they cheer,
In nature's concert that everyone hears.

A symphony styled with a wink and a nod,
In this patch of green where the growth is odd.
Laughter and music blend in the air,
Among leaves and blooms, without a care.

Resilience Amongst the Ancient Roots

In the garden, worms have a dance,
While daisies giggle with every glance.
The old oak tells jokes with a creak,
As squirrels debate who's the sleekest freak.

With roots like muscles, tough and bold,
They whisper secrets of days of old.
"Did you hear the one about the bug?"
The tree bark laughs, giving it a shrug.

A Breath of Fresh Fragrance

The flowers are gossiping, with petals so bright,
"Did you see that bee? He's quite the sight!"
Lilies in laughter; they sway and sway,
While roses roll their eyes, come what may.

A breeze dashes by, with a cheeky grin,
"What's the buzz, my flowery kin?"
The daisies erupt in a fit of mirth,
While tulips share who's got the best worth.

Whims of the Wind Among the Greenery

Oh, the wind is a prankster, tickling leaves,
Making branches dance like they just got thieves.
"Catch me if you can!" the zephyr shouts,
While trees quiver like kids with outsized doubts.

A gust whooshes in, plays tag with the sun,
While ferns giggle softly, having their fun.
"I'll spin you around!" the bramble yells loud,
As laughter bursts forth from the green, quite proud.

Rhapsody of the Awakening Branches

Branches stretch wide, in a comedic pose,
As if doing yoga, striking funny shows.
The buds pop out, sporting hats of surprise,
With twigs holding court under whimsical skies.

Chirping birds add to the hilarious air,
Singing their tunes with much flair to spare.
"Join us for brunch!" the leaves cry with glee,
As laughter erupts like a sweet symphony.

Reveries of the Resurgent Wild

When trees wear their hats of green,
The squirrels start to play unseen.
They dance like fools on branches high,
While birds just laugh and flutter by.

Bugs in suits parade along,
Each tiny creature sings a song.
They gossip 'neath the leafy shade,
And plot the pranks that they've displayed.

The flowers bud with silly grins,
While rabbits flex their furry chins.
Bees buzz around like tiny cars,
Weaving tales under the stars.

With every sprout a joke will bloom,
Nature's chuckles fill the room.
In this wild, a party's found,
As laughter grows from underground.

The Call of the Budding Branches

A twig just whispered, 'Hey, let's play!'
The buds pop up, hip-hip hooray!
With leafy wigs, they tip their hats,
As squirrels cartwheel, chasing rats.

The robins croon their wiggly tunes,
While dandelions don summer spoons.
Nature's jester with colors bright,
Turns the plain into pure delight.

The flimsy ferns do the cha-cha,
While thistles giggle, dadada.
Each branch a stage, each leaf a smile,
Frolic in fun, it's all worthwhile.

The sun peeks in, with a wink to say,
'Join the dance, come out to play!'
As buds rejoice and branches sway,
The world's a circus—hip hooray!

Life Springs from Silent Soil

In the ground where secrets dwell,
Earthworms feast at their own swell.
With laughter buried deep and grand,
They tickle roots with wiggly band.

Seeds gossip softly, old folks say,
'What's the weather like today?'
While mushrooms poke their heads and shout,
'We're the fun guys, come check us out!'

A cactus tries its hand at jokes,
While daisies giggle, nudging folks.
The soil hums a giddy tune,
A joyful party, morning noon.

Each sprout that peeks above the dirt,
Wears bright attire, as if to flirt.
In silent soil, the laughter grows,
As life erupts, in colorful shows.

Luminous Growth After the Quiet

From slumber deep, the garden stirs,
As blooms burst forth with silly purrs.
The tulips boast their vibrant hues,
While daisies play some game of clues.

With giggles hidden in the breeze,
The starlings chatter with such ease.
Each petal flutters, whispers bright,
In garden squares, a zany sight.

The sun comes bright, wearing a grin,
Inviting all the friends within.
The honeybees buzz like a choir,
As nature's joy begins to inspire.

And when the night drapes its dark cloak,
The moonlight bathes each playful folk.
With laughter echoing through the night,
The world stands still, all feels just right.

Sprouts of Promise in the Silence

In the quiet garden, seeds lay deep,
Dreaming of sunlight, and not of sleep.
Who knew that sprouts could dance and twirl?
With tiny leaps, they made the earth whirl!

A gopher giggled, peeking from below,
Watching the seedlings put on a show.
With wiggles and wobbles, they shook their leaves,
Perfecting their moves, doing handstands with ease!

The carrots wore hats made of leafy green,
While radishes twirled, a sight rarely seen.
Lettuce did cartwheels in bright summer sun,
Claiming the title of "Queen of Fun!"

Around the fence, the weeds rolled their eyes,
Thinking these sprouts were a silly surprise.
But laughter erupted, from stalks small and tall,
In this garden of cheer, they'd started a ball!

Moonlit Revelations in the Thicket

Under the moon, the branches hold tight,
Bunnies throw parties, oh what a sight!
The fireflies flicker like stars in a sway,
As owls spin tales of the prankster way.

A raccoon in shades plays the saxophone,
While hedgehogs groove, just chillin' alone.
Mice in tuxedos, with top hats on heads,
Swing dance through thickets, where mischief spreads!

The grass does the limbo, the roots stomp in tune,
As petals pirouette beneath a full moon.
Laughter erupts from each tiny beast,
For in the thicket, the fun never ceased!

With a wink and a nod, the night softly fades,
As morning brings whispers of secrets that stayed.
But the tales of that night will forever be found,
In the rustle of leaves, and the soft, cozy ground.

Vibrations of Verdancy

In a world alive with leafy lingo,
Plants gossip softly in fervent tango.
The daisies discuss their colorful dreams,
While the sunflowers plot to steal every beam!

A merry oak shakes off morning dew,
Telling the ferns they must join the crew.
Grass blades giggle, tickling their toes,
As daisies burst forth in a showy pose!

With roots tangled in a conga line,
Each sprout exclaims, "Let's sparkle and shine!"
A squirrel brings snacks—a buffet divine,
Encouraging all to sip sap like wine.

The fun never fades, just spins 'round the bend,
In this green jubilee, where we all blend.
So if you hear laughter when you're by a tree,
It's just nature's party, wild and free!

When the Seedlings Break Free

Amidst the soil, a ruckus unfolds,
Tiny sprouts chatting, breaking old molds.
"Let's ditch the darkness, let's stretch and sway,
We're off to see sunshine—it's a brand new day!"

With a pop and a crack, they burst from the ground,
Exclaiming their freedom with leaps and bounds.
"Who knew we were such great acrobats?"
The cucumber insists, flipping somersaults!

But watch out for raindrops, they slip and slide,
Making these spritzers want to glide.
A puddle forms, it's a splash zone for fun,
Where beetroot cannonballs make everyone run!

With each little sprout, mischief ignites,
Twirling and giggling, reaching new heights.
When the day ends, they snuggle and snore,
Dreaming of adventures, and what grows in store!

Secrets of the Thicket

In the thicket, squirrels conspire,
With acorns hidden, they con the choir.
A rabbit's dance, all eyes are wide,
As a hedgehog prances, a prickly guide.

Frogs flip-flop in a laughing spree,
While fireflies glow like a rave marquee.
The owls squawk jokes, oh what a scene,
It's the wildest party this side of the green!

Bushes gossip with rustling leaves,
Telling tales of the trickster thieves.
The fox might steal your last potato,
But don't you worry, he'll take you to the show!

Who knew nature had such flair?
With every bloom, a silly dare.
In every corner, laughter blooms,
As the thicket bursts with funny tunes.

Lullaby of the Leafy Embrace

Under canopies, the branches sway,
Whispering secrets in a leafy ballet.
Grasshoppers play a dreamy tune,
While crickets start their afternoon croon.

The leaves giggle in the gentle breeze,
As bumblebees take naps on the trees.
A sleepy owl yawns, with great big eyes,
Who knew the forest was full of surprise?

The flowers nod to the rhythm of night,
While fireflies twinkle, oh what a sight!
Buttercups chuckle, joining the fun,
In this lullaby, we're never done.

Every branch sways, every root twirls,
In nature's embrace, a rhythm unfurls.
The trees are the stars in this playful show,
A leafy lullaby that steals the glow.

Nature's Resurgence

With a wiggle and a giggle, spring's on the run,
Flowers explode, saying, "We're so much fun!"
Bees buzz around, wearing tiny hats,
While snails strut their shells like acrobatic brats.

The sun winks down, a mischievous spark,
Dancing with shadows in the park.
The trees stretch high, pulling silly faces,
As the breeze teases them through open spaces.

Rabbits hop with a jiggly cheer,
Their fluffy tails boast, "We're the best here!"
Even the daisies join in the race,
As they tumble about with a bright embrace.

Nature wakes up, oh, what a delight,
Bringing laughter and joy, morning to night.
In every nook, the humor flows,
As flowers bloom in ludicrous rows.

The Blooming Heart of the Forest

In the heart of the forest, where laughter runs wild,
The mushrooms twirl, acting like a child.
The raccoons are plotting a playful heist,
While the grumpy old owl feigns being nice.

The saplings dance as the breezes play,
With cheeky sunbeams that brighten the day.
Ladybugs giggle in their polka-dot wear,
While chipmunks juggle with absolute flair.

Bamboo sways, as if lost in a dream,
Making silly shadows that playfully beam.
The flowers gossip on the forest floor,
In a vibrant chat you can't ignore!

As night falls down, stars start to peek,
The forest reigns supreme, oh so unique.
With blossoms of joy, the laughter will last,
In this heart of the wild, a happy contrast.

Twilight Songs of the Sylvan Realm

In the woods, the squirrels dance,
Chasing tails, oh what a prance!
Every twig, a secret shared,
Whispered jokes—the trees all dared.

Moonlit beams on branches sway,
Mice in tuxedos join the play.
With a snap, a branch does fall,
Laughter echoes through it all.

Crickets tune their tiny bands,
While mushrooms play in fairy lands.
Twilight sings a cheeky tune,
Underneath the chuckling moon.

A raccoon wears a silly hat,
Inviting all for a late-night chat.
In the trees, the giggles grow,
As woodland folks put on a show.

Awakening Shadows on the Path

In the dawn, the shadows creep,
On glistening roads where willows weep.
Bunnies hop with floppy ears,
Chasing dreams without any fears.

A hedgehog reads a tiny book,
While drowsy owls just take a look.
Their hoots turn into silly songs,
As dancing leaves sway along.

The fairies jest with fluttering wings,
Telling tales of silly things.
A deer prances with comic flair,
Turning heads with all its hair.

In the grass, a lizard slides,
With a grin as wide as tides.
Shadows laugh and share their grace,
As morning sun joins the fun chase.

Glistening Dewdrops and Fresh Beginnings

Dewdrops hang on blades of grass,
Like tiny jewels, they shimmer and pass.
A frog sings opera on a leaf,
While rabbits dance in joyful disbelief.

Bumblebees buzz a funny tune,
Dancing 'round a sleepy June.
With every sip from flowers bright,
They wiggle in the morning light.

A caterpillar's wiggle makes a show,
As it munches on a leaf—oh so slow!
The world awakens with a grin,
And the sun chuckles as it spins.

Jolly gnomes with pumpkin hats,
Invite all critters, and even bats.
Laughter blooms amid the dew,
In this realm where antics brew.

Threads of Green Intertwined

Vines entwined, a wiggly dance,
Nature's party in a leafy trance.
Snakes wear ties made out of leaves,
While crickets hop in comic sleeves.

Silly squirrels trade acorn hats,
While rabbits bounce with gossip chats.
A fox slips on a slippery vine,
And tumbles down with a giggle divine.

Fluttering butterflies join the scene,
With dazzling wings of every sheen.
They twirl and whirl in the sunny air,
Making fun of the fluttering hair.

In this tapestry of green delight,
The woodland folks make each night bright.
With laughter woven in every thread,
They cherish joy in all they've said.

Murmurs from the Forest Floor

A squirrel once told a tree,
"I think I saw a bumblebee!"
The roots chuckled low and hearty,
As mushrooms joined the leafy party.

The grass danced with bits of fluff,
While acorns played it really tough.
Laughter echoed from the glade,
In nature's world, no charade.

The worms sang a silly song,
Tweeting birds joined right along.
Beneath the ferns, a foxes' prance,
Their antics led a merry dance.

With giggles from daisies that swayed,
The forest floor was not dismayed.
A tapestry of joyous noise,
A secret realm for all the toys.

Nectar of New Beginnings

Bees buzzing, what a sweet delight!
They whispered jokes throughout the night.
Pollinating dreams took flight,
With laughter that felt oh-so-right.

A hummingbird donned a bow tie,
Flew by and made the flowers sigh.
"What's nectar without a joke or two?"
He winked as he sipped the morning dew.

The petals laughed in colors bright,
As butterflies danced in sheer delight.
The budding trees prepared to play,
With every breeze, a joke to say.

In this nectar of vibrant cheer,
All creatures gathered, drawing near.
The sweetness spread, a rich delight,
In nature's love, all felt just right.

Rebirth Among the Branches

A clever crow wore a crown of leaves,
"A king for a day!" he chuckled, pleased.
The branches creaked, sharing a wink,
As young saplings dreamed and thought pink.

Furry critters jumped with glee,
While mockingbirds shouted, "Look at me!"
The canopy held stories galore,
Every branch a welcome encore.

The owls shared riddles under the moon,
While nighttime critters hummed a tune.
A raccoon tried to juggle some seeds,
Creating laughter from nature's needs.

Each leaf that rustled told a tale,
Of summer storms and autumn's hail.
Yet through it all, humor remained,
In the forest's heart, joy was unstained.

Twilight of the Eco-Realm

As twilight fell and shadows grew,
A turtle asked, "Why don't we glue?"
Then frogs croaked in playful jest,
"Glue? What's that? We know best!"

The sunfish told jokes to passing ducks,
While crickets tuned up their happy clucks.
Mice giggled in their tiny holes,
Sharing laughter among the knolls.

In the hush before the night took flight,
Every critter found pure delight.
The world was a stage, a fun-filled dream,
With nature's laughter, a joyous theme.

As stars twinkled with a cheeky gleam,
The eco-realm shared a whimsical dream.
What a magical way to end the day,
In every nook, creatures laughed and played.

Echoes of the Ancient Roots

In the garden, trees do chat,
Whispering secrets, how about that?
Squirrels gossip, all in jest,
With acorns dressed, they feel their best.

Roots that wiggle and twist around,
Making friends with worms underground.
The flowers laugh, a colorful crew,
As the daisies tease the violets too.

Beetles in bow ties, ready to spin,
Dance in circles, oh, what a grin!
The oak rolls its eyes, the pine starts to sway,
"Look at these bugs, they just want to play!"

But when the wind howls, they all hold tight,
"Stay close, my friends, it's quite a fright!"
With a rustle, they giggle as branches sway,
Nature's comedy in bright disarray.

The Dance of Leaves in Spring

Leaves do the tango, a vibrant sight,
Spinning and twirling, oh what delight!
Sunbeams chuckle, casting their glow,
As petals prance in the breezy show.

Grasshoppers hop, with moves so slick,
They leap and twirl with a little kick.
"Follow me, friends!" a leaf does shout,
And all join in, no room for doubt.

The breeze joins in, with a whoosh and a swish,
While butterflies swoop in for a wish.
Who knew plants could groove like this?
Nature's festival, we can't miss!

With laughter and joy, they sway all day,
In a leafy ball, they dance and play.
Each gust a giggle, each shake a tune,
As springtime laughter fills the afternoon.

Awakening Canopies

Canopies rustle, awake from their nap,
Chattering branches, a leafy clap.
"Rise and shine, let's stretch our limbs!"
As the sunlight beams, with joyful whims.

Birds serenade with a comical chirp,
While the clouds above do a little burp.
"Oops!" they giggle, as raindrops fall,
Turning the ground to a splishy-splash ball.

With puddles forming, the fun begins,
Kids jump in with loud whoops and spins.
Trees laugh along, shaking their leaves,
As mud-splattered shoes give nature reprieves.

"Catch me if you can!" a branch seems to say,
Twisting and turning as kids dance and play.
A joyful ruckus from ground to the sky,
Nature's all here for a riotous high.

Breath of the Verdant Dream

One sleepy seed in a dirt-filled bed,
Dreams of growing, pops up its head.
"I'll be the tallest, just wait and see!"
A sprout next door laughs, "You're tiny as me!"

In the sun's warm hug, they stretch so wide,
Creating shadows where critters can hide.
"Hey! There's room for a dance floor here!"
As ants march in, spreading all the cheer.

Up in the branches, the birds have a ball,
Playing tag and bouncing, never too small.
The leaves cheer loudly, waving with glee,
"Springtime's a party! Join in the spree!"

As the day rolls on, in laughter and fun,
The forest awakens, under the sun.
With giggles and wiggles, the life all around,
In the heart of the green, joy is profound.

Lively Ballet of the Budding Realm

In a garden where the flowers sway,
The daisies dance in bright array.
Worms wear hats, taking their turns,
As sunshine laughs and the humor burns.

Bees doing pirouettes in the air,
While butterflies giggle without a care.
A frog leaps in, doing the splits,
The tulips blush as everyone fits.

Rabbits bounce with comedic flair,
Critters applaud from right over there.
Each petal flutters, a joyful sight,
In this ballet, the world feels right.

Nature's Rebirth in a Whispering Breeze

A whisper sings through the budding trees,
Tickling leaves like a playful tease.
Squirrels chatter, planning their schemes,
While the daisies wake from their dreamy dreams.

The breeze pulls pranks on floppy hats,
As shy mushrooms share giggles with cats.
A puffy cloud joins the musical play,
Gliding along, in a frothy ballet.

Dandelions blow, spreading their jest,
Every flake floating north and west.
Nature chuckles, casting a cheer,
As flowers wink with a rainbow's veneer.

Spirits of the Timberlands Arise

In the timbers, where laughter roars,
The trees gossip behind wooden doors.
A wise old owl acts like a clown,
While mischievous raccoons run up and down.

The squirrels hold a nutty debate,
Arguing loudly about their fate.
The pinecones tumble, causing a fuss,
As nature smiles at this joyful bus.

Branches sway, shaking off grime,
Each twist a dance, each fling a rhyme.
Whimsical spirits in the woodlands play,
Turning the forest into a cabaret.

A Tapestry Woven of Sunlight

Sunbeams stitch a quilt in the air,
While flowers wear colors beyond compare.
A daffodil juggles, much to the crowd's cheer,
As bright little ladybugs chatter nearby, dear.

A playful breeze kicks up a fun chase,
Tickling petals in a soft embrace.
The sun winks at clouds, a cheeky facade,
While rainbows stretch, creating a facade.

Each morning's prank is a colorful scheme,
Nature's palette, a whimsical dream.
In this tapestry, laughter prevails,
As joy fills the air like fluttering sails.

The Forest's Gentle Resurgence

Trees stretch their limbs with glee,
   Squirrels plotting a wild spree.
  Leaves gossip on a sunny day,
    Nature's humor on display.

Buds burst forth with laughter sweet,
   While rabbits dance on tiny feet.
Mushrooms pop like wise-cracking gnomes,
   Claiming woodland as their homes.

The brook chuckles, splashing sounds,
   As playful breezes spin around.
  Old logs creak with tales to tell,
Of wacky friends who thrived so well.

A bunny wears a dandelion crown,
While ants parade in merry gown.
The forest bursts with silly cheer,
  A grand revival, loud and clear.

Beneath the Blooms

In the meadow where butterflies flirt,
Bees play tag in their sweet concert.
Petals giggle, dressed in bright hues,
While the daisies trade silly news.

A turtle races with hope and dream,
Waddling fast, or so it seems!
Frogs croak jokes from lily pads,
While ducks quack back, not even mad.

Beneath the blooms, laughter ignites,
Sunbeams dance in playful sights.
The wind tells tales of silly clowns,
While flowers wear their vibrant gowns.

With every step, a chuckle spills,
As nature plays with joyous thrills.
A patchwork of mirth in every shade,
Beneath the blooms, laughter's made.

Life Erupts

Oh, the chaos of sprouting seeds,
With a flair for funny misdeeds.
Worms wiggle and squirm in delight,
While ants march on, ready to fight!

A dandy lion wears shades of gold,
Telling tall tales that never get old.
Grasshoppers leap like they own the stage,
Chasing dreams in the sun's embrace.

The sunbeams giggle, tickling the ground,
As flowers bop to a rhythm they found.
A hedgehog snickers, rolling with pride,
In this wild, whimsical joy ride.

Life erupts in a harmless jest,
In nature's play, we find our best.
With every flutter, every chuckle bright,
The world joins in, a pure delight.

Dawn's Brush on a Leafy Canvas

Dawn splashes colors, oh what a sight,
Ticklish leaves are the morning's delight.
A fox peeks out, with a cheeky grin,
Wondering what mischief to begin.

Birds chirp in harmony, a lively ping,
While flowers yawn and stretch, take wing.
Ants chit-chat about their grand plans,
Throwing parties in the soil, no fans.

The sun moonwalks on branches and greens,
Painting shadows with funny routines.
A squirrel trips on a branch just right,
Creating giggles at morning's light.

Every corner holds a joyful prank,
In this leafy world, hilarity shrank.
With dawn's brush, the forest creates,
A canvas of laughter no one hesitates.

Traces of Forgotten Seasons

In the woods, where past seasons linger,
Silly signs point with playful finger.
A snowman now made of leafy clumps,
Whispers secrets of winter's jumps.

Fallen leaves dance like they own the show,
As squirrels chase shadows, giggling below.
The ghost of summer skip hops along,
Singing tunes of a woodland song.

A scarecrow grins, forgetting its fright,
Telling tales of the moonlit night.
With each rustle, a chuckle from trees,
Nature reminisces with playful ease.

Forgotten seasons weave a strange tale,
With laughter caught in the breezy gale.
Every trace a reminder of fun,
In this forest, where joy's never done.

 www.ingramcontent.com/pod-product-compliance
Lightning Source LLC
Chambersburg PA
CBHW071822160426
43209CB00003B/168